How to Fart on a Date

The Real Gassy Guide to Dating

with 101 Unique Dating Ideas.

Jon Tannen

First Edition: November 2024

DATING IDEAS

Dine at a Restaurant

You've just created a real lemon when the waiter stops by your table. Since it was a quiet one, ask the waiter if something has spoiled in the back (you know it has). Make sure to show sincere concern or your cover will be blown.

Go Dancing at the Club

You don't want your date thinking you've got the hottest booty in the club if it's a stinky one, so use your time wisely walking to the bar and exterminate those vapors with a few good shakes.

Go Ax Throwing

Be aware that throwing the ax could cause your under-air to be thrust out in a loud burst behind you, so be sure to clear the air before you kill the bear!

Visit a Dog Park

Ah, fresh air, exercise, and farty dogs in abundance. Take advantage of this gassy, green day and blame the dogs for any air pollution.

Go to a Cat Cafe

Did a cat just poop or is that your coffee breath? Who will ever know? Bring some gum to cover up your bad breath, along with an extra mint for the uprising below.

Enjoy Music in the Park

You can stand right next to your date, fart and they won't know it was you. That is, unless you accidentally add an extra drum beat during the music break.

Go Geocaching

Being outside is always a plus for your behind; just don't fart when your date is behind you.

Play Paintball

Team up with your date on this gratifying outing. When it's your turn to run and shoot, use some gas and propel yourself forward. It provides a huge relief and you won't be gearing up for an explosion later on.

Attend a Poetry Reading

Rhythms and rhymes take up the quiet space, so squeeze gently upon release, just in case.

Go to a Trampoline Park

Avoid any heavy foods beforehand because it won't take much bouncing before the pressure drops.

Take a Horse & Buggy Ride

There's nothing like taking a romantic horse
ride through the city. Plus, the horse's back
end will keep you in the clear since you'll be
competing with your rear.

Go Skydiving

If you're an adrenaline junkie who always
has the gas light on, this is the perfect date.
You can air out from top to bottom, as long
as your bottom stops before the ground.

Go Gambling

Noise won't be an issue here, and if you play in the smoking section, the strongest of smells won't be you.

Go to a Murder Mystery Dinner Theater

Your gas shouldn't become another mystery, so put on your fart pads and absorb the play.

Go to a Shooting Range

While keeping your pellets in, there might
be an urge to alleviate the extra pressure.
Just be sure to aim before you shoot out any
stink bombs.

Go to a Movie Theater

You'll be stuck in one seat at the theater, so
be sure to take a bathroom break to air out
your real thoughts about the movie.

Go on a Coffee Brewery Tour

No aftershave is needed to cover up mishaps on this date, since coffee is a natural deodorizer. That nutty smell will help rid unwanted emanations from the back garden before anyone notices the growth.

Visit a Planetarium

There's nothing like a little science to rocket you and your date to the moon. Since farts can only travel about 10 feet per second, you'll have to remain grounded. Instead, impress your date with some scientific knowledge about anything but flatulence.

Attend a Bake-Off

You'll be surrounded by yummy smells and good treats, and anything out of the ordinary can ruin an appetite. Try wearing some activated charcoal undies to absorb the extra spoils coming from your rump, so you don't spoil the day.

Go Roller-Skating

Roller-skating offers great air flow and a reason to hold your date's hand. On the other hand, any gas relief you have will only be temporary since you and your date will be skating right back into the cloud. Now that you know, be sure to use a different lane the next time you roll around to avoid any potential laughing gas.

Visit an Escape Room

Your gas won't have anywhere to go, so you may have to mask the beast behind you with some activated charcoal pants. You'll sacrifice a little style, but your butt will remain free.

Play at the Arcade

Practice your driving skills at a sit-down arcade game. It's loud and you can make simple adjustments from a comfortable, seated position.

Go Horseback Riding

You're riding down the trail and notice some low pressure building. Thankfully, the smell of horse manure is so overpowering that even your special body spray can't compete.

Go to a Drive-In Movie

Lay a blanket over your tailgate for some comfort and a quick filter. There's nothing like thick fabric to soak up the stench of the evening air. Plus, it'll keep things quiet on your end.

Play Laser Tag

You've got your gear on and you're ready to go; but that triple burger you ate earlier is causing some gaseous emissions. Now, go find a corner to hide in and let that fire out before it burns its way out.

Eat at a Breakfast Cafe

The countdown is on; the fart is near. Good thing you made the smart choice to order the eggs. Now it's anyone's guess if that special scent is you or the food on your plate. What a weird and smelly world we live in.

Play Pool

Whether you had wine or beer, there's going to be some noise back there. A quick bathroom break will help to relieve the pressure, but may not help you win the game.

Visit a Wax Museum

Okay, you've stunk up the place and wax doesn't smell. Point to any wax figure and say, "It was him!" Humor is your savior here.

Walk on the Beach

What a simple, romantic date idea. Thankfully, the wind is always blowing in two places - on the beach, and out of your butt.

Go to an RV Show

Check out those cool RV's! And what's that smell? It's not you. RV shows tend to bring in a certain generation. And that generation (we love ya) tends to be more gassy some experts have noted. So join the flow and let the exhaust fumes go!

Go to a Monster Truck Show

You'll score points if you bring extra ear plugs for your date. Yeah, it's that loud. And those fumes are no joke either. Speaking of gas, even a wind generator like yourself can easily become overpowered by a bigger engine.

Play Bingo

Bingo is a great game to win a little money and fart away your problems. There are a lot of butts in the seats too, so no matter which way your wind blows, nobody will call out your number.

Build a Snowman

Ah, building a snowman in that cool, crisp winter air is so refreshing… then there's you. Be strategic about getting away from your date for those special, extra crispy moments in the snow.

Volunteer at a Local Animal Shelter

The shelter already smells like poop so you're in the clear to be your gassy self. Plus, animals don't judge, but they do sniff.

Go to a Sports Game

There's a lot of cheeks in those seats, along with the air that goes with them. Whether you're standing up to cheer or eating a hot dog sitting down, practice the art of, 'Any fart, any time.'

Fly a Kite

You've got to love the wind; it carries kites and farts away like magic. Sometimes, all you have to do is let go.

Go Antiquing

Antique shops are known for that old, stale smell. So what's one more stale smell going to do? It might even blend into that vintage style you're going for.

Get Side-by-Side Massages

Overprepare to be relaxed. Go through the date preparation in the Before The Date section. If there was ever a time *not* to be gassy, this is it. You don't want to find yourself in a foul situation with a bloated gut.

Build a Fort and Watch a Movie

Grab those couch cushions, blankets and put
in a romantic movie. You'll need to leave
the fort for some bathroom breaks. If not,
you'll create a stink bomb and blow your
cover.

Go Fishing

If you're fishing, bring the smelliest bait you
can find. It will help cover up the fact that
your fanny is a farty fisher.

Play on Waterslides

Grab your swim trunks and climb up to the tallest slide. Now put your date in the front so you can blow up the tube all the way down.

Go on a Virtual Date

Eat all of the eggs you want before this date. But when it comes time to gas out, be sure to hit the button to mute yourself, and not the button to mute your date.

Watch a Rodeo

It already smells like manure and chili-farts,
so eat what you want and let 'em ride!

Go to a Comedy Show

Be careful you don't toot too loud in a
moment of silence, or the comedian will
roast your butt.

Visit an Amusement Park

Hop on a rollercoaster. Once you get going, you should be in the clear for a rear clean-out, but not a rare one.

Feed the Ducks

Buy duck pellets and go down to the lake. Between the breeze and that funky duck smell, any extra odors will fly away before your bottom drops.

Take a Botanical Garden Tour

The entire garden is like one giant bottle of air freshener; it'll make anything smell like roses.

Go on a Cider Mill Tour

You'll have the best hot cider you can imagine on this romantic daytime date. Plus, the aroma of the cider will overpower any hot visitors that come creeping up to the basement door.

Go Golfing

You'll have to say goodbye to your pride for a low-pressure game. When the gas creeps up, hook your next shot into the trees for some above-the-hole relief.

Tour a Corn Maze

Grab your boots and stomp around on the corn on this crunchy date. Be careful though, you may have to retrace your steps on the maize. Anything silent but deadly could be waiting around the corner with your name on it.

Go Go-Karting

Put the squeeze on your date when you make those tight turns. Then use the caution flag to cover your checkered past in the brake zone.

Go on an Art Walk

If you can keep your upper gas trap shut, you might make it to a second date. Any lower leakage is necessary to avoid a flare up.

Play Frisbee

Take your date down to the park and toss a frisbee. Along with getting exercise, you'll have all the space you need to run as fast as your wind can take you.

Go Kayaking

Fill up the empty space inside with gas and paddle down the river. Just don't back up during high winds, or your backside won't contain the leak.

Go on a Food Truck Tour

Plot a food course and pick your meals
wisely since walking and eating creates
extra gas. Or just for fun, throw caution to
the wind and have a couple of bean burritos.
It's your body!

Go Bowling

A lot of smelly feet, chili, and cheese dog
farts abound here. Go look for a new
bowling ball or get some food and let all the
fireballs roll on out.

Take a Pottery Class

Don't stand too close to the kiln when you
turn up the gas, you'll blow up your date.

Visit a Waterfall

Take a picnic and a dip near a waterfall.
There's nothing like thousands of bubbles to
cover up your own. Enjoy the swim and
don't hold back.

Take a Mixology Class

Knock the wind out of your date with a new,
fancy drink, not with the uprising below.
That's what the bathroom is for.

Go Scuba Diving

Check out the coral reefs and swim with the
fish. Stay behind your scuba partner to keep
those bum balloons from bursting in your
date's face.

Ride in a Hot Air Balloon

Speaking of hot air, you'll be waiting for the
perfect gust of wind to waft away that
backyard bouquet from your second
breakfast. Ah, romance is in the air.

Plant a Tree

You'll get a workout on this date and see
how well you work together. If any flowers
start to bloom, lean over and release those
seeds.

Go on a Brewery Tour

Sample a variety of beers on this relaxing
tour where carbonation is bubbling around
you. Just keep the drift outside of your draft
when the bubbles inevitably start popping.

Visit a Waterpark

Your date will be having so much fun they
won't notice the extra froth in the wave
pool. You know what they say, "All
bubbles, no troubles."

Visit a Comic Convention

You put on your favorite hero's costume and you're ready to party. Now squash any upcoming beasts with your superpower and slip back into the crowd.

Attend a Charity

While practicing being an awesome person, grab your date a drink and use that time to spread your cheer with other people at the event.

Go to the Opera

Pull on that pair of charcoal undies because there's no place to watch the opera and fart in peace. Let the underwear take the beating, not the people around you.

Go to an Indoor Rock Gym

Stay below your date on this aerobic rendezvous so you don't release any unwanted incense over your date's head.

Volunteer to Pick up Trash

Show some concern and volunteer in your community. While impressing your date, empty out the waste material into the garbage can, then clean up the trash.

Join a Swing Class

Get out those dancing shoes and learn some new moves. You'll be pressed to pay attention here so you don't step on your date's feet. Just be sure to keep the tempo during your swing, or your date might end up doing the polka.

Go Four-Wheeling

Whether it's sand, mud, or snow, you can usually find a good spot to show off your driving skills. And when it comes up, you can break the wind without breaking on your date.

Go on a Zipline

Take an exciting trip down the line with your date. Your hair won't be the only thing blowing in the wind on this adventure. Just be sure you don't cut the rope after you've cut the cheese.

Take Salsa Lessons

Keep things spicy with some exciting salsa lessons. You'll have a blast with your date dancing the mambo; just don't blast off before the date ends.

Visit a Flea Market

You may have gotten wind that your date enjoys a good bargain. Since flea markets have a certain, musty smell, your backyard barbecue might liven things up a bit. Share the joy with others and grab those deals while they're hot.

Eat Ice Cream

You may not be cutting the cheese here but there will be dairy involved. Prepare yourself with a lactase enzyme before you sprinkle any extra sweets onto your date.

Make a Sand Sculpture

Grab a bucket and some carving tools for this creative date. While showing off your skills, sit down and filter out the ocean's froth before the tide comes up.

Play Tennis

Sweat out that date anxiety with some physical activity. Make sure you wear your strongest deodorant; you can use it in many places.

Go Birdwatching

Grab a bird book or open a birdwatching app on your phone. Find and identify the birds you see and keep the chirping in the back down to a minimum.

Visit a Museum

There's nothing like the love of old things to inspire a new relationship. Your local museum is a tour through history. Just keep the future rosy, and don't double-back where the old vapors flew.

Go Chalking

Buy some multi-colored chalk and prepare to become an artist of the street (or sidewalk). Since there will be a lot of drawing and bending over, use that time wisely to squeeze out any nagging tension caused by being so creative.

Go on a Dessert Walk

Map out a tour of dessert shops for you and your date. From warm ice cream to frosted donuts, you'll each feel like a kid again. Be sure to keep the dairy down to a minimum for a minimum of dairy farts. That way, you can focus on tasty treats and not your hindquarters.

Visit an Aquarium

Check out the vibrant sea life at your local aquarium. Take some photos and have some fun. Keep an eye out for the mammal behind you though, or you might get more crap than you deserve.

Go Sledding

Your butt bouncing down the hill won't help
to keep the gas pellets in, so relax, lean
back, and ride that breeze all the way down.

Attend a Book Reading

Use the restroom before it starts so you can
get away from the quiet space before the
wind knocks down the shelves.

Karaoke

Take the stage and air out your grievances
from top to bottom. Just keep the
microphone away from any bellowing
below.

Ride Scooters

If you're riding together, remember the seat
will only absorb so much pressure. So ease
off the gas and you'll be off to the races.

Go Swimming

You're both out enjoying a nice summer lake swim. The sun is warm and so is the breeze. Suddenly, you feel a heaviness coming up from behind. It's pressing. Release the tension with some spring action and let the wind take your troubles away.

Visit a Zoo

When you're walking through the large animal section, you'll be in the clear to clean yourself out without the smell giving you away.

Take a Ferry Ride

Stand on the deck for some great air flow
and check out the landscape. Even when
your pipes are deflating, your date will be
none the wiser.

Listen to Live Music

Have a blast listening to some great tunes at
a live show. Just keep the blast radius away
from your date's nose, or the other explosion
might be on you.

Go Sailing

Keep the wind at your sails because this is the ultimate date. Whether you're raising the mainsail or dropping anchor, the gale winds you create won't make your date take the dinghy home.

Rent a Convertible

Take a scenic tour on a rural back road and let your worries fly away. If anything warm comes up for a visit, you can give it a swift goodbye with one simple press of a button.

Play Mini Golf

Grab a club and show off your golfing skills.
Be sure to avoid the double bogey when
your turn comes up. Otherwise, your date
might be blown off the green.

Go on a Photo Shoot

Put on vintage clothes and get some
photographs taken. Just don't make any
straining faces while the pressure is being
relieved, or it will remain in history forever.

Go on a Scavenger Hunt

Take an interactive tour of your town on a scavenger hunt. You'll catch up on local history and discover some mysteries along the way. Win the most points by finding the most items and you'll be on your way to a win. Just be sure to keep any extra visitors outside so the next search party doesn't come looking for you.

Go Bicycling

Tuck in your laces and show off those calf muscles. You might even want to join a cycling club for this little adventure. Just be sure to let your date take the front so you can exercise your right to express yourself in the back.

Go to a Farmer's Market

Fresh food, music, and local artists are a treasure in any town. Pick up some fragrant flowers for your date and you'll score romance points while tamping down the pungent odor coming from your blossoming behind.

Go to an Archery Range

Cupid's arrow will be at play here. When it's your date's turn to shoot, don't let your butt become the target of an unexpected projectile.

Play Pub Trivia

Toot your own horn with some fun bar trivia. Your date will be impressed with your knowledge, and you can slip out the thunder from down under with ease.

Take a Ghost Tour

Go on a spooky adventure that will take you and your date to your city's most haunted places. Hold your date's hand as you tour these scary sites and listen to frightening stories of the past. Don't get too spooked though, or something might pop out of the shadows and surprise the crap out of your date.

Go Apple Picking

Pick yourself some apples, but don't pick
your nose. Don't pick anything else unless it
smells like a rose.

BEFORE THE DATE

Don't Smell like a Fart

Instructions:

1. Go number two.
2. Wash bum thoroughly, preferably in the shower.
3. Put on clean underwear and clean pants.
4. Give yourself a look in the mirror for that special seal of approval.

Wear Activated Charcoal Clothing or Fart Pads

Buy activated charcoal products to keep your under-armor scent-free. Whether it's underwear, pants, fart pads or chair cushions, have some fun with it.

Farting is a Hairy Business

The more bum hair you have in the farting area, the quieter your fart can be. The opposite is also true. Prepare yourself accordingly.

Do Pre-Date Yoga Exercises

Some yoga poses release gas build-up. One of the best-known poses for wind relief is the Pawanmuktasana pose. You've got this!

Avoid Carbonation

If it doesn't get burped out, you'll be farting it out. You're aware of those bubbles, right?

Poop First

If you know it's going to happen during the date, get something to help it along beforehand.

Use Cologne or Perfume

Just don't submerge your date's nose in it, even if *you* think it's great.

Know your Gassy Foods

These are: dairy, beans, fruits, meats, and carbonation. More specifically, foods such as red meat, eggs, onions, and garlic will give you smellier farts, and more of them.

Make sure you pay attention to what you eat ahead of time so you don't scare away your date the first time.

IF SOMETHING COMES UP

Leave Something in Your Vehicle

Oops, you "forgot" something you needed from your car. Go grab it and push that gas out. Just don't bring it back in with you.

Situation: Bowel

Feeling flushed? Go to the restroom. It may seem obvious, but if your butt is talking over you and your date, give it a break. It needs to vent. Remember, listen to your body - your butt is a part of it and shouldn't be left at the bottom.

Situation: Constipation

Lean forward on the toilet and relax your sphincter. Prepare to let go.

Situation: Silent but Deadly Attack

You're sitting across from your date at the restaurant when your backdraft becomes deadly, really deadly. Don't panic. Just ask your date if they need a bathroom break. This may make it awkward for a moment, but go on as if nothing happened.

Situation: Walking Farts

Practice the sidewalk gas-pass. Whether its people talking or a loud car going by, be a side-wind opportunist.

Situation: Laughing Gas

This is the innocent laugh-and-fart. You're sitting with your date and realize a fart is creeping its way up. If you have a joke or funny story, now is the time to tell it. The best part of this is the perception that farting while laughing is seen as more funny than gross. It can be a silly story you both can look back at later on.

Situation: The Purposeful Fart

If you really like this person, you have the option to do an overt test fart on the first date. Now don't go crazy here, the fart alone should not be what breaks the ice. This test fart is great for one thing - finding out if there will be a second date. If there is, it probably means the person is really into you (or has completely lost their sense of smell, which is also promising).

Situation: Share the Blanket

It's easy to turn a blanket into a fart pad. Just pile up some of the blanket behind your backside, then let 'er rip.

Situation: The Tie-and-Toot Method

Prepare for this method by wearing shoes with laces. When the time is right, bend down and tie your shoes for a better chance at a quiet fart.

Situation: Your Date Farts

Don't look at your date. When you go on as if nothing happened, you'll surely be on your way to a second one.

Situation: Farting in the Car

Unless the windows are down, your fart will be noticed. Instead, absorb that stench with some activated charcoal pants. They look like regular pants but have the superpower of neutralizing the malodorous odors you produce.

Made in United States
Troutdale, OR
12/15/2024

26414551R00040